THE INDIANAPOLIS COLTS

BY KIERAN DOWNS

EPIC

BELLWETHER MEDIA ★ MINNEAPOLIS, MN

EPIC BOOKS are no ordinary books. They burst with intense action, high-speed heroics, and shadows of the unknown. Are you ready for an Epic adventure?

This book is intended for educational use. Organization and franchise logos are trademarks of the National Football League (NFL). This is not an official book of the NFL. It is not approved by or connected with the NFL.

This edition first published in 2024 by Bellwether Media, Inc.

No part of this publication may be reproduced in whole or in part without written permission of the publisher. For information regarding permission, write to Bellwether Media, Inc., Attention: Permissions Department, 6012 Blue Circle Drive, Minnetonka, MN 55343.

Library of Congress Cataloging-in-Publication Data

Names: Downs, Kieran, author.
Title: The Indianapolis Colts / by Kieran Downs.
Description: Minneapolis, MN : Bellwether Media, 2024. | Series: Epic. NFL team profiles | Includes bibliographical references and index. | Audience: Ages 7-12 | Audience: Grades 2-3 | Summary: "Engaging images accompany information about the Indianapolis Colts. The combination of high-interest subject matter and light text is intended for students in grades 2 through 7"-- Provided by publisher.
Identifiers: LCCN 2023021966 (print) | LCCN 2023021967 (ebook) | ISBN 9798886874792 (library binding) | ISBN 9798886876673 (ebook)
Subjects: LCSH: Indianapolis Colts (Football team)--History--Juvenile literature. | Baltimore Colts (Football team)--History--Juvenile literature.
Classification: LCC GV956.153 D68 2024 (print) | LCC GV956.153 (ebook) | DDC 796.332/640977252--dc23/eng/20230518
LC record available at https://lccn.loc.gov/2023021966
LC ebook record available at https://lccn.loc.gov/2023021967

Text copyright © 2024 by Bellwether Media, Inc. EPIC and associated logos are trademarks and/or registered trademarks of Bellwether Media, Inc.

Editor: Betsy Rathburn   Designer: Gabriel Hilger

Printed in the United States of America, North Mankato, MN.

TABLE OF CONTENTS

A BIT OF LUCK	4
THE HISTORY OF THE COLTS	6
THE COLTS TODAY	14
GAME DAY!	16
INDIANAPOLIS COLTS FACTS	20
GLOSSARY	22
TO LEARN MORE	23
INDEX	24

A BIT OF LUCK

ANDREW LUCK

The Colts are playing the Texans in the 2018 **playoffs**. Colts **quarterback** Andrew Luck throws a pass. It is caught for the **touchdown**!

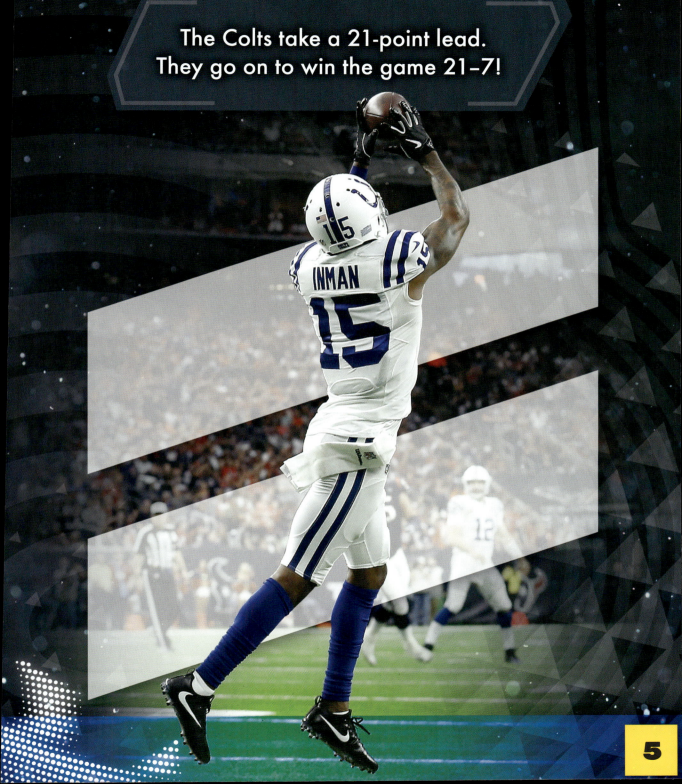
The Colts take a 21-point lead. They go on to win the game 21–7!

THE HISTORY OF THE COLTS

The Colts began in Baltimore, Maryland. They joined the National Football League (NFL) in 1953.

Quarterback Johnny Unitas led the team in its early seasons. He helped them win the NFL **championship** in 1958 and 1959.

1953 COLTS GAME

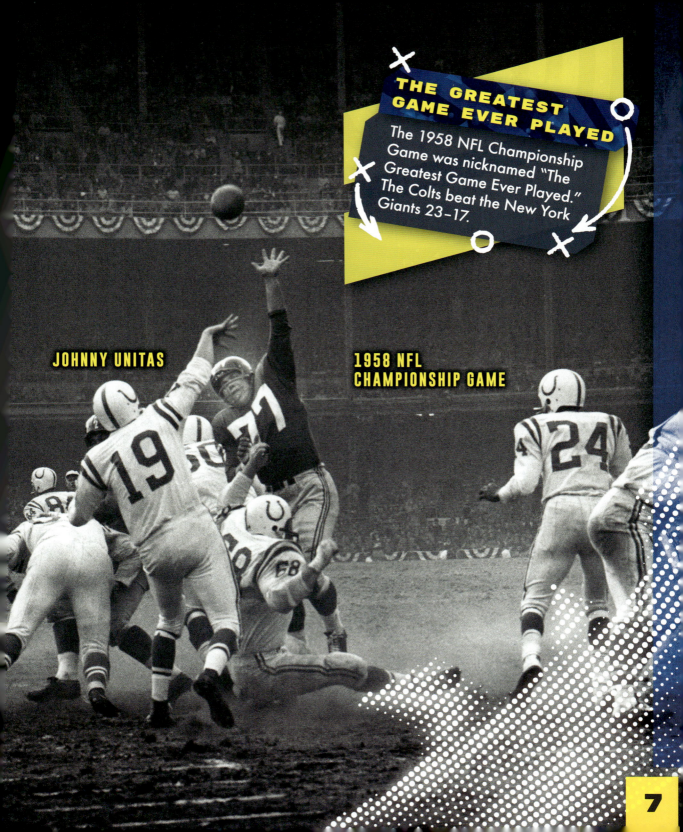

THE GREATEST GAME EVER PLAYED

The 1958 NFL Championship Game was nicknamed "The Greatest Game Ever Played." The Colts beat the New York Giants 23–17.

JOHNNY UNITAS

1958 NFL CHAMPIONSHIP GAME

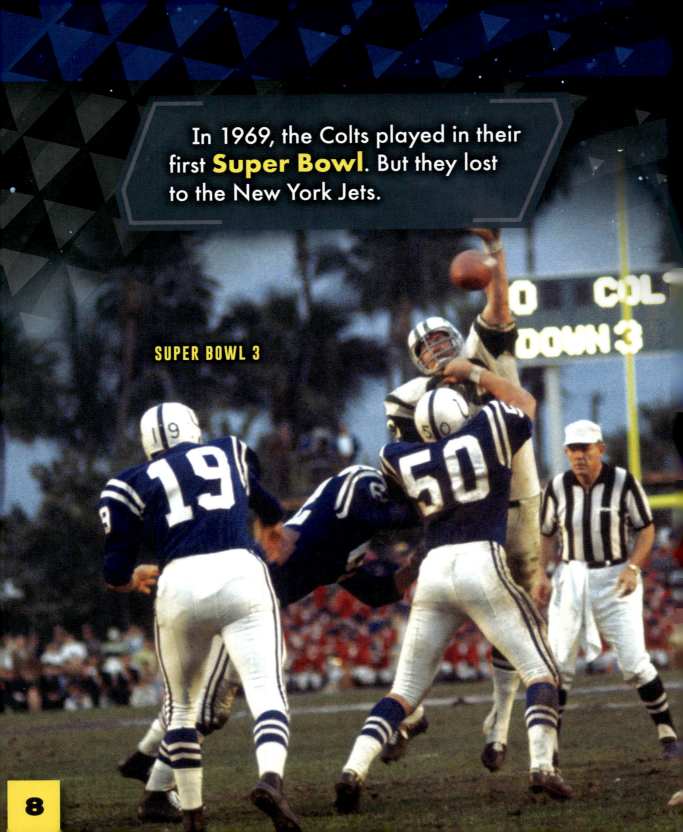

In 1969, the Colts played in their first **Super Bowl**. But they lost to the New York Jets.

SUPER BOWL 3

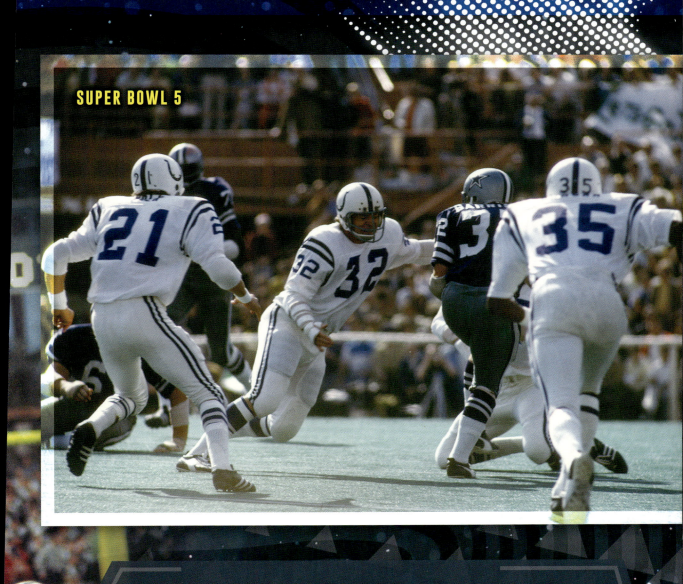

SUPER BOWL 5

Two years later, the Colts returned to the Super Bowl. They beat the Dallas Cowboys for their first Super Bowl win!

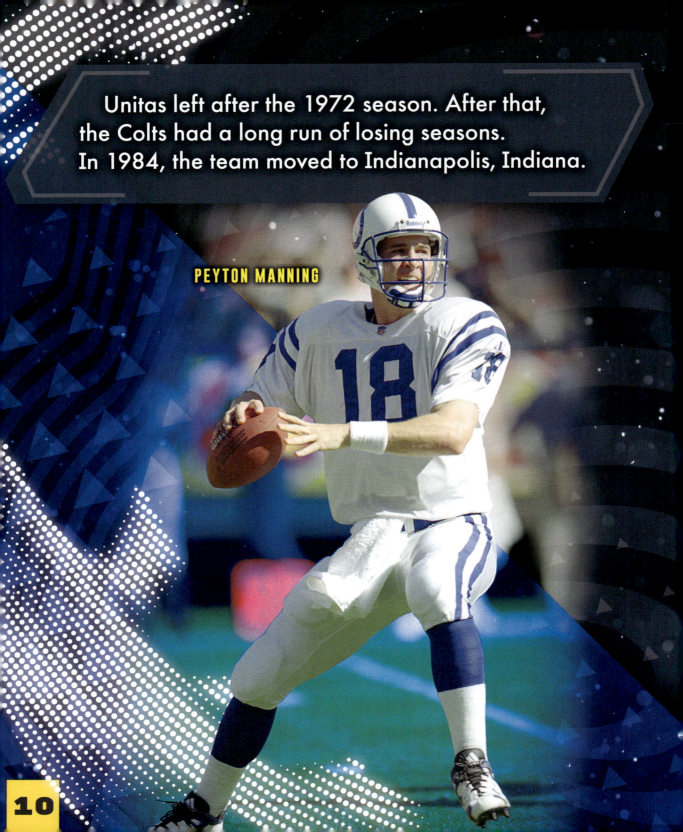

Unitas left after the 1972 season. After that, the Colts had a long run of losing seasons. In 1984, the team moved to Indianapolis, Indiana.

PEYTON MANNING

The Colts continued to struggle. In 1998, quarterback Peyton Manning joined the team. He helped bring more wins.

🏆 TROPHY CASE 🏆

AFC SOUTH championships: 9

AFC championships: 3

SUPER BOWL championships: 2

NFL championships: 3

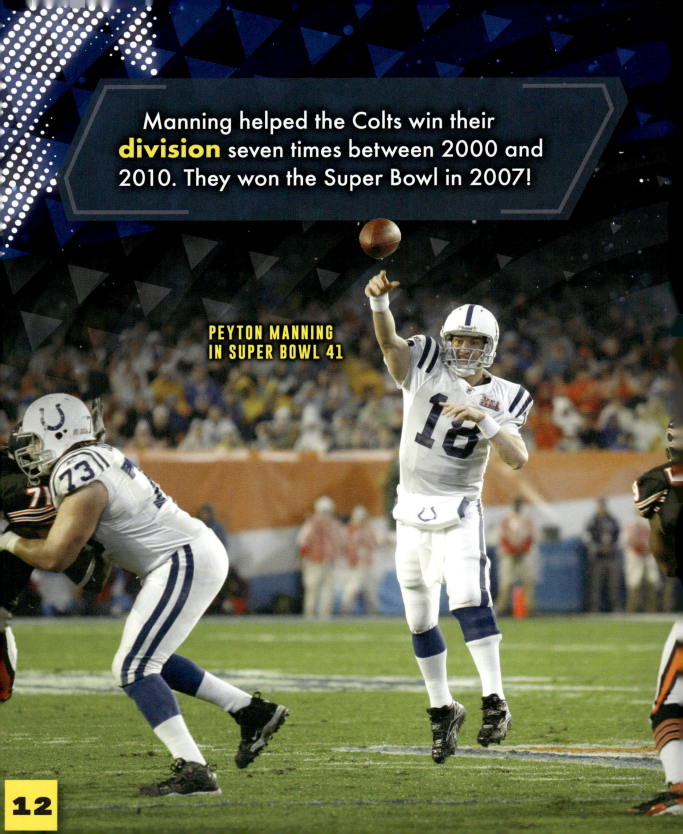

Manning helped the Colts win their **division** seven times between 2000 and 2010. They won the Super Bowl in 2007!

PEYTON MANNING IN SUPER BOWL 41

The Colts reached the playoffs five times in the 2010s. The team looks forward to more wins in the future!

POINTS LEADER

In 2018, Colts kicker Adam Vinatieri set the NFL record for most career points. He finished his career with 2,673 points. He scored 1,515 with the Colts!

THE COLTS TODAY

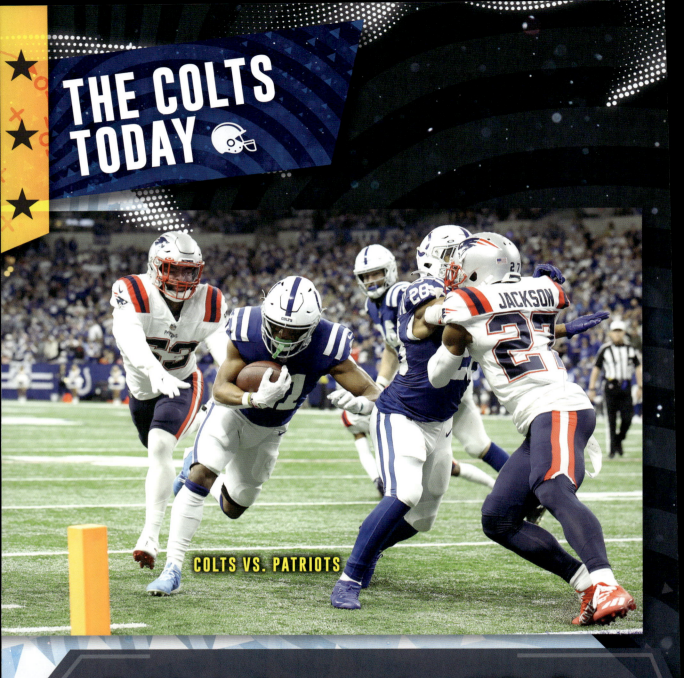

COLTS VS. PATRIOTS

The Colts play their games in Lucas Oil **Stadium**. It is in Indianapolis, Indiana.

The team plays in the AFC South division. Their biggest **rival** is the New England Patriots.

 LOCATION

LUCAS OIL STADIUM
Indianapolis, Indiana

INDIANA

GAME DAY!

Colts fans often gather to eat and party before games. They dress in blue and white. Many wear jerseys of their favorite players. Blue is the team's **mascot**. He helps fans cheer for the team.

GOOD LUCK CHARM

Blue became the team mascot in 2006. That season, the Colts won the Super Bowl!

BLUE

A fan or player bangs a large **anvil** to start home games. A loud horn sounds when the Colts score touchdowns.

Colts fans love to root for their favorite team!

ANVIL

★ FAMOUS PLAYERS ★

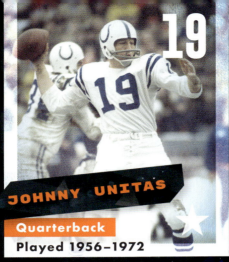

JOHNNY UNITAS — 19
Quarterback
Played 1956–1972

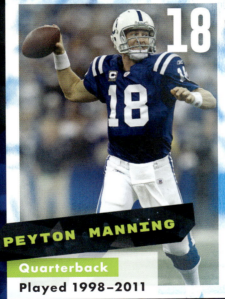

PEYTON MANNING — 18
Quarterback
Played 1998–2011

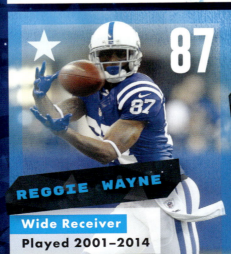

REGGIE WAYNE — 87
Wide Receiver
Played 2001–2014

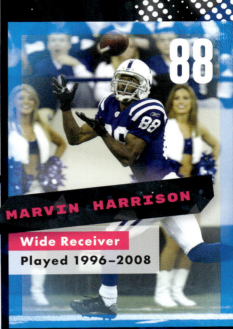

MARVIN HARRISON — 88
Wide Receiver
Played 1996–2008

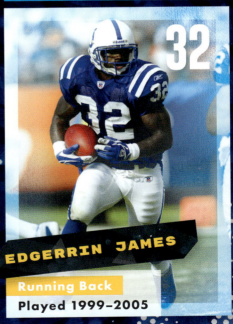

EDGERRIN JAMES — 32
Running Back
Played 1999–2005

INDIANAPOLIS COLTS FACTS

LOGO

JOINED THE NFL	1953

MASCOT
BLUE

NICKNAME	The Shoe

CONFERENCE
American Football Conference (AFC)

COLORS

DIVISION | AFC South
- Houston Texans
- Jacksonville Jaguars
- Tennessee Titans

STADIUM

★ LUCAS OIL STADIUM ★
opened August 16, 2008

holds **70,000** people

20

🕒 TIMELINE

1953 The Colts play their first season

1984 The Colts move to Indianapolis

2007 The Colts win their second Super Bowl

1971 The Colts win their first Super Bowl

1998 Peyton Manning joins the team

★ RECORDS ★

All-Time Passing Leader | **All-Time Rushing Leader** | **All-Time Receiving Leader** | **All-Time Scoring Leader**

Peyton Manning — 54,828 yards
Edgerrin James — 9,226 yards
Marvin Harrison — 14,580 yards
Adam Vinatieri — 1,515 points

GLOSSARY

anvil—an iron block on which metal is shaped

championship—a contest to decide the best team or person

division—a group of NFL teams from the same area that often play against each other; there are eight divisions in the NFL.

mascot—an animal or symbol that represents a sports team

playoffs—games played after the regular season is over; playoff games determine which teams play in the championship game.

quarterback—a player whose main job is to throw and hand off the ball

rival—a long-standing opponent

stadium—an arena where sports are played

Super Bowl—the annual championship game of the NFL

touchdown—a score that occurs when a team crosses into their opponent's end zone with the football; a touchdown is worth six points.

TO LEARN MORE

AT THE LIBRARY

Cooper, Robert. *Indianapolis Colts*. Minneapolis, Minn.: Abdo, 2020.

Goodman, Michael E. *Indianapolis Colts*. Mankato, Minn.: The Creative Company, 2023.

Leed, Percy. *Peyton Manning: Most Valuable Quarterback*. Minneapolis, Minn.: Lerner Publications, 2022.

ON THE WEB

FACTSURFER

Factsurfer.com gives you a safe, fun way to find more information.

1. Go to www.factsurfer.com.
2. Enter "Indianapolis Colts" into the search box and click 🔍.
3. Select your book cover to see a list of related content.

INDEX

AFC South, 12, 15, 20
anvil, 18
Baltimore, Maryland, 6
colors, 16, 20
famous players, 19
fans, 16, 18
history, 4, 5, 6, 7, 8, 9, 10, 11, 12, 13, 17
Indianapolis, Indiana, 10, 14, 15
Indianapolis Colts facts, 20–21
Lucas Oil Stadium, 14, 15, 20
Luck, Andrew, 4
Manning, Peyton, 10, 11, 12
mascot, 16, 17, 20
National Football League (NFL), 6, 13, 20
NFL Championship Game, 6, 7
nicknames, 7, 20
playoffs, 4, 5, 13
positions, 4, 6, 11, 13
records, 13, 21
rival, 15
Super Bowl, 8, 9, 12, 17
timeline, 21
trophy case, 11
Unitas, Johnny, 6, 7, 10
Vinatieri, Adam, 13

The images in this book are reproduced through the courtesy of: Cal Sport Media/ Alamy, cover; Sean Pavone, cover (stadium), p. 15 (Lucas Oil Stadium); Zuma Press, Inc./ Alamy, pp. 3, 18-19, 21 (2007); Perry Knotts/ AP Images, p. 4; Tim Warner/ Stringer/ Getty, p. 5; Vic Stein/ AP Images, pp. 6, 21 (1953); Robert Riger/ Contributor/ Getty, pp. 6-7; Focus On Sport/ Contributor/ Getty, pp. 8, 9, 19 (Johnny Unitas), 21 (1971); G. Newman Lowrance/ AP Images, p. 10; Kevin C. Cox/ Contributor/ Getty, pp. 12-13; Icon Sportswire/ Contributor/ Getty, pp. 13, 20 (mascot); Andy Lyons/ Staff/ Getty, pp. 14, 19 (Peyton Manning), 21 (Edgerrin James); NFL/ Wikipedia, pp. 15 (Indianapolis Colts logo), 20 (Colts logo, Texans logo, Jaguars logo, Titans logo, AFC logo); Stacy Revere/ Stringer/ Getty, p. 16; Michael Hickey/ Contributor/ Getty, pp. 16-17, 21 (Adam Vinatieri); Gregory Shamus/ Stringer/ Getty, p. 19 (Marvin Harrison); Allen Kee/ Contributor/ Getty, p. 19 (Edgerrin James); UPI/ Alamy, p. 19 (Reggie Wayne); Carol M. Highsmith/ Wikipedia, p. 20 (stadium); Al Messerschmidt Archive/ AP Images, p. 21 (1984); Jamie Squire/ Staff/ Getty, p. 21 (1998, Marvin Harrison); PCN Photography/ Alamy, p. 21 (Peyton Manning); Bob Levey/ Contributor/ Getty, p. 23.